DREAMS

DREAMS

EVELYN M. YOUNG

ELEMENT

Shaftesbury, Dorset • Boston, Massachusetts • Melbourne, Victoria

© Element Books Limited 1998

First published in Great Britain in 1998 by
ELEMENT BOOKS LIMITED
Shaftesbury, Dorset SP7 8BP

Published in the USA in 1998 by
ELEMENT BOOKS INC.
160 North Washington Street, Boston, MA 02114

Published in Australia in 1998 by
ELEMENT BOOKS
and distributed by Penguin Australia Ltd
487 Maroondah Highway, Ringwood, Victoria 3134

Designed and created with
The Bridgewater Book Company

ELEMENT BOOKS LIMITED
Managing Editor *Miranda Spicer*
Project Editor *Finny Fox-Davies*
Production Director *Roger Lane*
Production *Sarah Golden*

THE BRIDGEWATER BOOK COMPANY
Art Director *Peter Bridgewater*
Designer *Stephen Parker*
Managing Editor *Anne Townley*
Project Editor *Caroline Earle*
Picture Research *Vanessa Fletcher*
Studio Photography *Heather McDonough*
Computer Illustrations *Ivan Hissey*
Endpapers *Sarah Young*

British Library Cataloguing in Publication data available

Library of Congress Cataloging in Publication data available

Printed and bound in Italy by Graphicom S.r.l.

Picture credits:
Bridgeman Art Library, London: cover (main pic) (L. Russolo: Music/Musée Grenoble),
6 (British Museum), 19 (Museum of the American Indian, NY), 46 (Jesi Coll, Milan).
e.t. archive: cover bl, 15.
Games System Inc., U.S.A.: 32–33.
Images Colour Library/The Charles Walker Collection: cover ml, 8–9, 17, 27.
The Stockmarket/ZEFA: cover (tl, mr, br), 10, 18, 22, 36, 40, 51.

ISBN: 1-85230-254-3

CONTENTS

DREAMS IN HISTORY

Dreams were traditionally interpreted in myth and legend as messages from some other world, which could cure illness or foretell future events; but they also provide insight into our emotional preoccupations. They have featured in dramatic works from Shakespeare's plays to Hollywood scripts, and in paintings from Hieronymus Bosch to Stanley Spencer.

THE FASCINATION OF DREAMS

 We take it for granted that a dream can illuminate a fabricated story, yet we often fail to recognize that our own real-life stories – the things that are happening to all of us, every day – are also more clearly seen in the light of our dreams.

Today we don't think these insights are anything to do with messages from other worlds. Instead we find that in our fast-moving lives, while our circumstances and relationships may change too quickly for our conscious mind to grasp what is really happening, our subconscious mind often reveals the truth as we sleep. But long before we learned this, human beings treated dreams as supernatural messages.

All creatures dream. But why? Since the beginning of recorded history, the mystery has remained unresolved.

BABYLON AND EGYPT

 As civilizations spread throughout the eastern Mediterranean, both the Babylonians and the Egyptians came to revere Jews as interpreters of their dreams. The Bible contains the famous account of the dream of Nebuchadnezzar, the Babylonian king, that was bravely interpreted for him by the Jewish folk hero, Daniel. In the book named after him, the Bible reveals Daniel to have been a skilled seer and interpreter of visions and dreams.

A 3,000-year-old papyrus from Egypt reveals that priests devoted to dream interpretation were called the Scribes of the Double House. Believers arrived at the temple to sleep, where they took a potion, and, on awakening, their dreams were interpreted and a cure prescribed.

ANCIENT GREECE

 In Ancient Greece, priests administered drafts to induce dreaming sleep from which a troubled or sick person would awaken healed. Hypnos was the sleep-inducing god. He carried the sleeper into the arms of Morpheus, who would communicate warnings and prophecies, or Aesculapius, who applied soothing snakes to lick the sleeper better.

THE BIBLE TELLS HOW DANIEL INTERPRETED THE DREAM OF NEBUCHADNEZZAR.

THE CLASSICAL WORLD

The dream-interpreter was both therapist and confessor in ancient Greek society, and then as now, the credulous were vulnerable to exploitation by unscrupulous charlatans. A certain cynicism set in. Intelligent observers such as Plato (c. 429–347 B.C.E.) and Aristotle (c. 384–322 B.C.E.) noticed that the physical state of a person could affect dreams, and tried to bring a more reasoned approach to the mystery of why dreams happened; but such cynicism made little impact.

ARTEMIDORUS MADE AN EARLY ATTEMPT AT DREAM ANALYSIS.

Artemidorus, writing in the second century C.E., published five volumes of dream interpretation that made the collected wisdom of the ancient world available to an educated class throughout the Mediterranean.

THE DARK AGES

The early Christians declared that the Church could be the only possible conduit for messages from God. Influential Christians such as the Italian St. Jerome (died 420 C.E.) alleged that dreams were messages from the Devil. The Church's authority was as vulnerable as its leaders feared. In the seventh century of the Christian era, the prophet Mohammed claimed that the Koran had been dictated to him in a dream.

THE MIDDLE AGES

In the Middle Ages the commentaries of Thomas Aquinas (an Italian scholar) attempted to combine Aristotle's scientific rationalism with Christian doctrines of faith and revelation and these views still represent the dominant thinking of the Catholic

Church. Clearly, there was no room here for the language of dreams. But in India, Hindu mystics compiled a kind of dream dictionary, and copies of this reached northern Europe where they were sold in the fairs and bazaars, despite Church disapproval.

In the sixteenth century when those suspected of practicing magic could still be tortured or put to death, dream dictionaries continued to circulate. They even became respectable, with the social rise of necromancers such as Simon Forman and Dr. Dee.

RATIONALISTS AND ROMANTICS

 In the intellectually curious spirit of the English Civil War period, Artemidorus's five volumes were reprinted in England in 1644. There followed rationalist attempts to ignore dreams as unimportant or, at best, some kind of physical symptom.

Romantic visionaries such as Blake and Goethe, whose dreams were seminal to their art, led the backlash against rigid rationalism at the end of the eighteenth century.

THE VICTORIANS

 By the mid-nineteenth century, science had begun its triumphal progress. Perhaps in reaction, Victorian literature produced a genre of horror and dream fiction, M. R. James and Edgar Allan Poe, two of its best known writers, taking the dream experience to move the story along. Lewis Carroll's *Alice in Wonderland* has been described as an extended dream. These authors led the way for fantasy literature in our own time.

CARROLL'S *ALICE IN WONDERLAND*.

SIGMUND FREUD (1856–1939)

 Near the end of the nineteenth century, Sigmund Freud, an Austrian physician specializing in psychiatric disorders, began to examine and interpret the dreams of his patients. The medical establishment was skeptical but Freud insisted that dreams were "the royal road to the unconscious." He claimed that the human mind operated on three levels: those of the Id, the Ego, and the Super-Ego.

The Id is the unconscious pleasure principle driving us to act as we desire; the Super-Ego is the restraining voice of society, our parents, and our conscience. The Ego, the conscious mind, mediates in this conflict between greedy Id and severe Super-Ego. The result of this conflict is the outward expression of our personality.

Freud perhaps over emphasized the eroticism of many dream images but he believed that by studying a person's dreams he could uncover what, in their Id or unconscious, was so overwhelmingly powerful. In dreams these things would rise to the surface, to be seized and examined by the analyst.

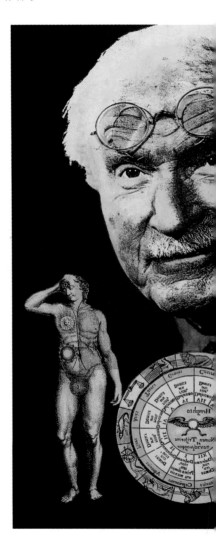

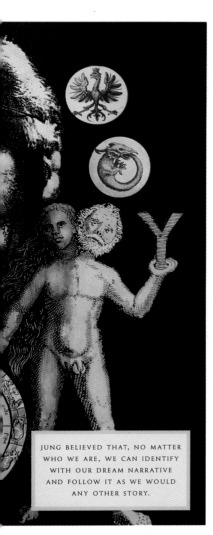

JUNG BELIEVED THAT, NO MATTER WHO WE ARE, WE CAN IDENTIFY WITH OUR DREAM NARRATIVE AND FOLLOW IT AS WE WOULD ANY OTHER STORY.

CARL GUSTAV JUNG (1875–1961)

We all dream; almost all verte-brates dream, and it seems unlikely that we're all fighting back revelations of deep trauma or lust. Freud's one-time disciple, Carl Gustav Jung, suggested an alterna-tive hypothesis. Underlying the Ego, the Super-Ego, and the Id was another layer of consciousness, which he called the collective unconscious.

Jung had noticed that dreams, throughout history and all over the world, tend to have a narrative structure. This structure contains images, figures, and experiences, which Jung called archetypes, that we can all share and understand because they have common characteristics which communicate a universal truth to the dreamer. These archetypes are there to alert us, by means of a parable, to some aspect of our lives of which we might otherwise be unaware (see pages 32–33).

Unlike Freud, Jung was prepared to believe that the meaning of a symbol could vary according to the dreamer. Listening to dreams was not a case of "listening to reason" but was a delicate, intuitive matter.

WHAT ARE DREAMS?

In the early 1950s, researchers showed that sleep is not a static condition. Adult human beings sleep according to predictable cyclic rhythms that, drawn as a diagram, look like lengthening waves.

SLEEP PATTERNS

 The Dream-time mainly takes place during the seven or eight bouts of REM (rapid-eye-movement) sleep that occur every night. The typical sleep cycle commences with a 40-minute descent, through four physical stages, to "deep sleep" followed by a brisker rise to a 10-minute REM stage in which the brain is active while the body remains entirely still. This is followed by another descent and rise to a longer REM stage. As the seven or eight hours of sleep progress, the waves subsequently lengthen to about 100 minutes and the REM stage to about 30 minutes.

PHYSICAL CHANGES

 Electrical impulses that are produced by the brain can be measured, and instruments connected to the sleeper's face and body muscles record other changes. These include:

✳ STAGE ONE

Slow breath, low heart rate, low body temperature, low blood pressure, and no eye movement; the sleeper is not hard to awaken at this stage though brainwaves are slow.

AS WE SLEEP, WE EXPERIENCE SEVERAL STAGES OF SLEEP PATTERNS IN APPROXIMATELY 90-MINUTE CYCLES.

✳ STAGE TWO

Bursts of high frequency brain-waves interrupt slower ones; sleeptalking and sleepwalking may occur now.

✳ STAGE THREE

Large and slow brainwaves. There are no eye movements.

✳ STAGE FOUR

Largest, slowest brainwave, regular breathing.

✳ REM SLEEP

Irregular breathing, muscular twitching, increased heart rate, and rather higher blood pressure and oxygen consumption. The body is still except for the eyes, though the brain is as active as during wake-fulness. It is difficult to wake up directly from REM sleep.

The emotions induced by our dreams may cause physiological change in, for instance, the amount of gastric acid or tears we produce. Yet because muscle tone is so low, and inhibitors are being produced to prevent action, no obvious physical reaction is observed.

Momentary awakenings are common throughout stages one to four, and can be minutes long. We are generally unaware of them, although sometimes we may suddenly recall having answered the phone in the middle of the night. These awakenings can signif-icantly reduce the amount of sleep we actually have.

It is at least as important to dream as it is to sleep. However, sleep is not merely the guardian of our dreams, for during slow-wave sleep certain hormones are secreted for growth and regeneration.

DREAMING AT DIFFERENT AGES

 Babies are in REM sleep for half their sleep time. Infants and pubescent children need to spend up to two-thirds of sleep time in REM sleep. An adult spends about a quarter of sleep time in REM, or "emergent" sleep, and slightly more as old age approaches.

If you don't get enough REM sleep, your body will compensate with more at the next opportunity. Insufficient REM sleep causes disturbance in normal daytime behavior, as dream images thrust themselves into the waking consciousness.

In a 70-year life span, five or six years are spent in REM sleep. A 24-week fetus is in REM sleep the whole time. Is it, in any sense, dreaming? Nobody can be sure.

CHILDREN'S DREAMS

 Like adults, children have wish-fulfillment dreams, but unlike adults, they have no autonomy, so the natural frustrations of powerlessness may emerge in "bad dreams."

Children sometimes have nightmares about being chased or eaten. This may be a metaphor for being subsumed into the personality of another, stronger person. They also dream of carrying out acts of aggression; a revenge fantasy, perhaps – but before you jump to horrified conclusions, ask what they were watching on TV or reading the day before.

DURATION OF DREAMS

 Dreams compress narrative, as movies and books do, and in real time take about as long as they seem to in dream-time – ten to 30 minutes at roughly 90-minute intervals. Oddly, our attention span in waking life also seems to slump every 90 minutes or so. It is as if we are watching a series of short films throughout the night and snoozing in between.

CHILDREN OFTEN SUFFER FROM NIGHTMARES, COMMONLY ABOUT BEING CHASED OR EATEN BY MONSTERS OR FEROCIOUS ANIMALS.

GESTALT AND OTHER DREAM THEORIES

Fritz Perls (1893–1970) thought everything we dream reveals our own self or our own life events. This is the shape (gestalt) of the individual, rather than any collective unconscious. The gestalt can best be examined through role-play, for all the characters in the dream represent parts of oneself that may need to be confronted or questioned. Integration of all parts of the personality is the point.

Médard Boss (born 1903) takes an existentialist approach to dream interpretation and theory. Existentialism argues that each individual chooses, whether consciously or not, what he or she wants to be. The wish-fulfillment aspect of the dream is significant and may be obvious. For it is argued that just as we construct our dreaming life as individuals, so we construct our own personal waking life, each of us defining our world as we go along; we live, not as collective animals, but within autonomous bubbles of consciousness.

THE LATEST RESEARCH

Since a scientific breakthrough in the early 1950s enabled us to identify exactly when during sleep most dreaming takes place, the reasons for dreaming continue to cause speculation. Recent solutions include an analogy with a computer, in which dreaming is a kind of "disk housekeeping" for the brain; useless stuff is dumped and other

REM SLEEP ACCESSES THE INTUITIVE RIGHT BRAIN.

information filed away; no insight is to be gained by recalling the process. Another theory is that dreaming evolved simply as a way for animals to remain vigilant while asleep, as their brains awaken intermittently.

This book takes a less dismissive view, and will outline the possibilities of dream-reading for self-analysis and problem solving.

RIGHT BRAIN
AND LEFT BRAIN

The human brain consists of two hemispheres, right and left. Neuroscientific investigation has shown that the hemispheres perceive the world in slightly different ways: while the left brain is verbal, analytic, and deliberate, the right is rapid, intuitive, more visual, and symbolic, and can make unexpected creative connections. REM sleep, prompted by a chemical released from nerve fibers, is mainly right-brain.

Creative artists can access their right brain functions more easily than most people. In our dreams, as in art, we find a visual and emotional "reality" that may bear no logical reference to time or space.

ARTISTS PLUG INTO THE
CREATIVE RIGHT-HAND
SIDE OF THE BRAIN
MORE FREQUENTLY
THAN OTHER PEOPLE.

HYPNOGOGIC AND HYPNOPOMPIC SLEEP

 Hypnogogia is the semi-dreaming state we drift into just before we go to sleep, and hypnopompic sleep occurs as we start to wake up.

Hypnogogic sleep can be visionary; we may envisage archetypal faces or pure colors, or even experience acute, god-like insights into our own life situations. These are usually visions of great clarity, rather than narratives from which we can draw inferences.

Hypnopompic dreams tend to be somewhat disjointed. They may persist into wakefulness as creative solutions to a particular problem, or simply as a strong sense of direction; these dreams tend to be grounded in present reality.

PARASOMNIA

 Parasomnia – usually sleep-walking or night terrors – is a disorder of sleep stage transition. It takes place during Stage Two sleep, and typically sleep-walkers emerge directly from it (with no transitional REM sleep) having been awakened by some internal mechanism as yet unknown to us. Ask a sleepwalker and you may find that they can recall a dream they were acting out; this seems to confirm that dreams may take place during stages other than REM sleep.

The theory that the brain is "seeing" the dream like a movie seems to be borne out by experiments. Observers noticed that one woman was clearly in REM sleep, except that her eyes were not moving. On awakening she told them she had been watching a horse-race – on television, at a distance.

TELEPATHIC AND PRECOGNITIVE

 Certainly people do foresee the true winners of horse-races in dreams, though there are probably even more dream-winners that stagger last past the post in real life. Somebody some-where has usually foreseen a natural disaster that occurs – but then, with the entire population dreaming six or seven times a night, the odds are that someone would.

Although evidence suggests that telepathic dreaming sometimes occurs in close relatives, no reliable means of controlling or inducing dream telepathy – or indeed precognition has yet been found. Experimenters have observed telepathic communication under laboratory conditions but inducing it has always had variable results and has been less than enlightening.

DREAMS AS A PARALLEL OF OURSELVES

 Freud saw dreams as nature's way of revealing an unresolved conflict deep within the patient. Nowadays we are more likely to see an interactive system, a "transaction" going on in the mind between our outer personality and the intuitive perceptions we so often deny. Such transaction may have nothing to do with observable reality, although by analyzing what our dreams have to show us we can make better sense of everyday life.

FREUD BELIEVED THAT WE BURIED UNRESOLVED CONFLICTS DEEP WITHIN OUR UNCONSCIOUS, BUT THAT THESE SUPPRESSED EMOTIONS WERE REVEALED IN OUR DREAMS.

DREAMWORK IN GROUPS

As Freud pointed out, the brain condenses, displaces, symbolizes, and disguises its true perceptions: however, little by little, we can learn to decipher the true hidden meaning of a dream.

THE LISTENING GROUP

 Aboriginal communities in Malaya, Australia, and North America still use communal dream-telling as a ritual. Dream interpretation does not have to be the province of a priestly caste; anyone can do it, and one way is to

set up your own group of five or six interested people to work together.

Every member of the group is at some stage "the dreamer;" every dreamer is sometimes a "listener;" members of the group tell their dreams, then the others respond to these images as if they were their own dreams. Ideally the group should act as a therapist, listening, never offering an interpretation but by subtle questioning lead the dreamer to deeper self-analysis.

The group's purpose is not to pass judgment. Its members should empathize, that is, try to visualize the dream from the dreamer's point of view.

DREAM-TELLING IS AN IMPORTANT PART OF AUSTRALIAN ABORIGINAL RITUALS.

Try to find out the dreamer's own opinion of what the dream had to tell them. If they have no idea, try to find out whether there is any over-riding current preoccupation, with money or relationships or career, for instance, to which the dream could be referring. Gentle questioning may encourage the dreamer to look at certain aspects of their life that they had perhaps unconsciously put to one side, or tried to ignore.

Then look at each aspect of the dream in turn. This is the Jungian "amplification" technique. Ask what each symbol and person, sound and action, means to the dreamer. Take nothing for granted.

While it may seem obvious to you that a sunny field full of daisies is a pleasant setting, the dreamer may associate it with some frightening event, such as receiving bad news or having a violent quarrel. Ask "What does this particular setting mean to you?"

One advantage of group work is that the group may be the first to see a pattern in the dreams of the individual. However, offer your own

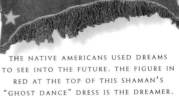

THE NATIVE AMERICANS USED DREAMS TO SEE INTO THE FUTURE. THE FIGURE IN RED AT THE TOP OF THIS SHAMAN'S "GHOST DANCE" DRESS IS THE DREAMER.

theories to others only if you are asked to, and be prepared for a defensive reaction. Most importantly, allow that you may be wrong. Remember that you may not be in full possession of all the details.

THE REVEALING DREAMER

 If you intend to present your dream to a therapeutic group for discussion and analysis, you will have to be totally honest – not only about the dream, but about the circumstances of your life. Your defenses should come down completely, so don't choose a group where you feel uncomfortable or in which you sense any desire to judge, patronize, or bully you.

It's not a good idea simply to relate your dreams to friends. Other people's dreams can be tedious, and even your best friends may stifle a yawn.

If you are asked anything about the dream you don't want to answer fully, try not to lie and at least be honest with yourself about what your dream has revealed.

Rather than relying on a plodding set of symbolic meanings, the dreamer who trusts their own intuition to interpret dreams is most likely to find new perceptions through dreamwork.

If the meaning of your dream is not illuminated by the group's questions, ask them for their own ideas.

Don't be irritated if the answers seem way off target; the group isn't in such full possession of the facts as you are. It is more than likely that you will gain something, however, from seeing your dream from another person's angle.

NEVER THE SAME AGAIN

 The closest one can get to the truth about a dream is the account written immediately upon awakening. Although it can never match the spontaneous excite-ment of the dream itself, a virtually on-the-spot commentary, read aloud, has to be taken very much more seriously than any dream that is recollected after several hours of distracting wakefulness.

The metaphors and unconscious puns, the visual detail and deeply felt emotion, of the dream fade rapidly. Also, Freud noticed, we tend to make "secondary revision" to the narrative in recounting it to somebody else; we hide what we don't want to see.

Some therapists argue that a dream recounted is essentially a right-hemisphere experience trans-lated into a left-hemisphere, verbal form. That is to say a symbolic and intuitive experience becomes analyzed and verbalized; a pale shadow of the visual dream experience that rarely has the emotional impact of the original. Others set great store by the words we use to describe our dreams, which can give away a great deal.

GROUP WORK MAY HELP US GAIN A REWARDING AND BENEFICIAL INSIGHT INTO OUR DREAMS.

ACTION

 An action plan can be worked out when we have new insights from our dreams. Secret ambitions or sorrows are laid bare; the true nature of relationships and belief-systems becomes apparent; repressed conflicts and anxieties over dependence, commitment, or abandonment are revealed.

LEARN FROM
YOUR DREAMS

It is a physiological fact that everybody dreams, even though you may be one of the millions who hardly ever remember what they dream about. Yet sleep can be more fun and more productive than you have ever suspected. You can train yourself to remember dreams by keeping a written record of all your dream experiences in a dream diary.

RECURRING DREAMS

The easiest dreams to learn from are those that recur. In waking life, we'll learn almost anything as long as it's repeated often enough, and our right brain seems to be programmed to communicate on this assumption in sleep, for there is no escaping from a recurring dream until its message has been understood.

LUCID DREAMS

A lucid dream is one in which the dreamer is conscious of dreaming. Few of us have any control of this phenomenon but it

has happened to most of us from time to time. Having kept a dream diary for some time, you may wish to train yourself to have lucid dreams more often.

Hindu mystics have claimed that lucid dreams can become so vivid that we can really be in two places at once, that is to say, traveling in body as well as in the mind, in a way that is apparent to others around us.

THE DAY RESIDUE

Most of us have found mental detritus from the previous few days in our dreams. That doesn't necessarily confirm the brain-as-waste-disposal theory.

The image may be as insignificant as a shaft of sunlight gleaming on a teacup, but even if it barely registered at the time, there is no guarantee that it won't play a major part in the nighttime drama. The right brain, like any imaginative artist, seizes whatever happens to be around as a useful metaphor or a symbol. You will find that the day residue seems to act on top of layers of emotion that are already in place.

SOMETIMES, EVEN IN THE MOST INDISTINCTIVE DREAMS, A SHARP DETAIL WILL REMAIN IN THE MEMORY.

23

KEEPING A DREAM DIARY

You have to catch dreams, as they fade fast, and are not at all the same experience in "lifeless memory." Very few people write their dreams down quickly enough. Make sure you record them immediately on waking.

KEEP YOUR DREAM DIARY IN AN EASILY ACCESSIBLE PLACE BY YOUR BED.

It is amazing how much more sense dreams make if they have been recorded at once; but this requires a lot of practice. Even if your brain wakes you up in astonishment at the insights you've had, your body wants to get a good night's sleep. You are leaden. It seems impossible to open your eyes, put the light on, and start writing.

A little folk wisdom works here. Exactly how we can thump our heads seven times on the pillow and awaken at precisely 7:00 A.M. is unclear, but most of us can. Our waking selves can pass instructions to our sleeping selves; we can tell ourselves, as we drop off to sleep, to remember our dreams.

The dream diary is a dedicated, special notebook. If you want to write tomorrow's Things To Do or the definitive plot point in your screenplay, write them elsewhere.

If all else fails, and you can't drag yourself awake enough to write in your diary, try murmuring your dream into a tape recorder.

If awakening your partner at regular, annoying intervals would make a dream diary impossible, then do your best to record your dreams as soon as possible after you have woken up in the morning.

---

* *Keep a lamp, the dream diary, and a pen by the bed.*

* *As you go to bed, write the date on a fresh page. This will let you check any developing themes.*

* *As you go to sleep, remind yourself how much you are looking forward to the insights your dream-experiences will give you.*

* *If you wake up in mid-dream, and catch yourself thinking "must write that down in the morning" – stop. Put the light on, sit up, and write it all into the diary: every detail.*

* *Be precise. Be comprehensive. Record as much information as possible. Include everything you saw and heard including names of people or places in the dream. Write in the present tense. Describe your emotions and mood exactly.*

* *Switch off the light and go straight back to sleep.*

AFTERGLOW AND AFTERGLOOM

The most important thing about the dream is the emotion it makes you feel. Dreams may make you wake up giggling; they can motivate and help you to visualize your innermost desires. Remember those dreams, for they have shown you the possibilities.

 Dreams can fill you with a sense of despondency or foreboding. When these kind of dreams occur you are giving yourself a warning: "Pay attention," you're saying, "and deal with this situation." So sit down and analyze the bad dream's real meaning.

A dream of something fearful is nature's way of telling you to come to terms with your fears and confront a problem. You have to be prepared to admit "I dreamed of my sick father dying alone because that's what I'm afraid of," or "I dreamed of burglars breaking into my home because I fear that someone else is going to invade my life and disturb it."

Have your deepest fears any real substance? Remember that the greatest fear of all is fear itself. Should you spend more time at your father's sickbed? Should you cancel your invitation to your boyfriend to move in with you, or simply relax and learn how two people can live together?

About a day after you have drawn your conclusions, double-check. Go back and look once more at the dream-diary record. You may find fresh significance in the words you used and may even conclude that the dream wasn't about those preoccupations that you have identified, but about an entirely different problem. Perhaps someone is:

* *afraid to let go?*

* *finding it hard to communicate?*

* *refusing to acknowledge something?*

* *refusing to recognize something for what it is?*

* *refusing to utilize the talents they have?*

* *afraid of change?*

* *afraid of failure?*

* *afraid of being held back?*

* *carrying a burden of shame?*

If nothing seems to cast light on the problem, and by now you have become expert at lucid dreaming, you may wish to try recreating the dream. You know you can change the ending; most of us have at some stage changed the ending of a dream from "inside." Once inside the dream you will see those small details which, by alteration, will change a negative outcome to a more positive one.

FEARFUL DREAMS ARE OFTEN NATURE'S WAY OF WARNING YOU TO CONFRONT A PROBLEM.

INTERPRETATION

The dreaming mind communicates its messages using many of the symbolic images that were identified by Sigmund Freud and his successors.

THE LANGUAGE OF DREAMS

 The language of dreams has common themes and widely accepted meanings. To interpret your dreams you will need to be familiar with the symbolic language of dreams. Once you understand the common symbolism it is easier to interpret your dreams according to your own experience.

CONDENSATION

Concentrating characteristics in a symbol of an archetype such as a wise man or judge.

DISPLACEMENT

Here, the dreaming mind dare not express itself, but instead produces a variety of images that are heavy with sexual symbolism.

REPRESENTATION

An idea represented as an image. A person who feels left out in some way may literally dream of being shut out of a building in which others are safe.

VERBAL METAPHOR

Insight and inspiration sometimes echo the commonest verbal metaphors. A literal dream funeral may in fact refer to a figurative real-life situation.

PUNS

Look for verbal word games in your dreams. A salesman frantically pedaling his bicycle in his dream could, in real life, be experiencing difficulty "peddling" his product.

SEXUAL DREAMS

Sexual wish-fulfillment dreams often have a deeper meaning than the obvious and you should analyze the participants and the roles they are playing carefully.

THE TIME FRAME

Dreams that take place in the historical past or the future may be trying to tell you something too brutal or socially unacceptable for you to accept if located in the present.

THE PLACE

We visit places in our dreams which we have never been to in life. Dig into your psyche to find out why.

PROBLEM SOLVING

 Having learned the relevance of last night's dream to your present concerns, such as money worries or relationships, you may find you have a more solid grasp of the true situation than you knew yourself capable of.

Problem solving by dream analysis has been a reality for thousands of years. Scientists, inventors, and novelists have solved many a problem by sleeping on it – essentially, waiting for the answer to rise through the dream.

In 1983 Morton Schatzmann set two brainteasers in Britain's Sunday Times *and asked for overnight solutions, which he got. Several people went to sleep thinking of the problem, and awoke suddenly knowing the solution.*

These revelations do not come from another world but from within. You know "the solution" at some very deep level. Listen to your dreams; they have a lot to tell you.

THE DREAM LANDSCAPE

Insight and inspiration are not necessarily communicated from dream-life to waking life through language. We "see" what dreams mean. Dreams are visual metaphors from the right-brain level.

IMAGES IN DREAMS

According to dream researchers, men, women, and children have very different dreams. Men tend to populate their dreams with male figures and very physical themes or images such as cars, sports, or machinery. Women, on the other hand dream of relationships and houses, and children report dreaming consistently about animals or frightening monsters. To make matters even more complicated, visual metaphors mean different things to different people.

The range or scope of dream images varies because they are drawn directly from our personal memory banks. Read an old dream dictionary, and you will find there references to homely objects and plants most of us have never seen, far less dreamed of. By the same token, our ancestors didn't dream of watching computer screens.

Despite this fact there are a number of images or themes which commonly appear in dreams, such as water, nudity, time, falling, flying, drowning, climbing, and chasing or being chased. Archetypal dream figures are explained on the following pages, and some of the most common dream themes have been highlighted in boxes or appear on pages 42–43, as anxiety dreams. The following chapters outline other dream metaphors that are common and the kind of meanings they have. This is not a dream dictionary, but a guide to the possible meaning of what you see.

DREAMS VARY WITH AGE AND SEX. MALE
THEMES INCLUDE PHYSICAL SPORTS WHILE
WOMEN DREAM MORE OF RELATIONSHIPS.

✦ ARCHETYPAL DREAMS ✦

*Archetypes are common figures thrown up by our subconscious that convey
a universal truth. Each archetype has a negative and positive aspect,
both masculine and feminine, and their function is to help us explore
our feelings, sensations, intellect, and intuition. Archetypal dreams
involve monster and myth, strange landscape, and time and place shifts
that are rationally impossible; they have that cosmic overview
that we can see in the work of the Surrealist painters.*

KINDLY MOTHER AND DESTRUCTIVE MOTHER

These archetypes convey the positive and negative aspects of femininity. One represents the nurturing, loving, forgiving mother figure, the other, the kind who suffocates and manipulates through a controlling love.

KINDLY FATHER AND OGRE

The two sides of masculine sensation are vividly conveyed in the dream world by a man who can care for us with loving and just authority and the dominating, despotic, aggressive, and downright frightening monster.

PRINCESS AND YOUTH

The princess and the youth are the gentle and carefree male and female sides of our personality. They have a childlike spontaneity and love of life.

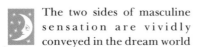

SIREN AND TRAMP

 Negative feelings are vividly conveyed by the vagrant who wanders from place to place, without any thought for others but only for what he can get from life. This is also true of the self-absorbed enchantress who is only too aware of her powers to seduce.

HERO AND VILLAIN

 The hero, as a positive representation of the male intellect, suggests a man who is entirely in control of his own destiny but who is prepared, if necessary, to do the greater good in achieving his goals. The villain, on the other hand, is a negative image, entirely egocentric and self-seeking, and will walk all over others in pursuit of his own glory.

AMAZON AND COMPETITOR

 The Amazon is the independent and self-reliant career woman who thrives on intellectual stimulation. Her negative counterpart, the competitor, feels the need to vie with everyone in order to prove that she is in control.

PRIEST AND PRIESTESS

 The priest and priestess have highly developed powers of intuition. They see through to the essential truth behind every thought or deed. The priest will use this knowledge in the service of a higher being, while the priestess will use her powers wisely in order to benefit humanity.

SORCERER AND WITCH

 The negative aspects of intuition are inherent in the sorcerer, who exploits his ability simply for the sake of it and revels in his power to do so. Occasionally he can become trickster and is capable of the completely unpredictable. The witch employs her skills entirely for her own ends.

COLORS

In dreams, colors are often so vivid that you know they are playing an important part in the narrative. Although there are conventional meanings for colors, be wary of attributing someone else's interpretation to an experience that is uniquely your own.

BLACK

 To see black clothing in a dream usually signifies something unpleasant, though not necessarily a death or funeral. Black often means things that are unknown, that are buried deep in the subconscious and can suggest that the dreamer may be experiencing an emotional trauma.

RED

 Red is a color we normally associate with anger and violent emotion, but it can also mean forceful energy, strength, virility, and life itself. Spiritually, it is the color of self-image and sexuality.

GREEN

 The color green suggests growth and expansiveness, a very positive sign. To meet someone in a dream dressed in green hopefully signifies prosperity and happiness for the dreamer. Green is the color of self-awareness.

YELLOW

 To see someone wearing yellow in a dream could imply approaching happiness and prosperity. A modern interpretation of the color yellow is peace and harmony. Yellow is the color of the emotional self and connotes thinking, and intellect.

ORANGE

 Orange is seen as a combination of yellow and red with their qualities of peace and energy. It represents relationships.

COLORS EACH HAVE THEIR OWN SPECIAL QUALITIES AND PLAY AN IMPORTANT PART IN OUR DREAM NARRATIVES.

BLUE

 To meet someone wearing blue indicates that you are moving toward a victory in some sense. Blue usually indicates happiness but, in the context of a mood, it could mean depression or "the blues." It represents self-expression and wisdom and is the primary healing color.

WHITE

 This color used to be associated with approaching sadness, but modern interpretations favor white for truth, spiritual purity, and protection. It is the color of innocence.

BROWN

 This is the color of earth and it may indicate that the dreamer should return to basics, to insure their feet are firmly on the ground. It is the color of commitment.

PURPLE

 The color purple is spiritually uplifting, suggesting divine protection, nobility, and hope.

LANDSCAPE

Every dream is played out against a backdrop but sometimes this landscape is just background scenery, sometimes it is an integral part of the dream itself that reflects our feelings and our personality.

TREES

 The tree is symbolic of our personality and spiritual development. If the tree is bare and thin, it indicates low self-esteem; if large with wide branches, a warm, welcoming nature; if pruned or manicured, a well-ordered, structured personality.

FORESTS

 If you enter a dark or enchanted forest, you are entering the spiritual world, your soul needs to be tested in order for you to fully comprehend your own nature. If you get lost in the forest, you have literally lost your way in life and need to take a grip on yourself.

DESERTS

 A desert is a barren landscape, a place of abandonment and desolation, and, although one old dream dictionary indicates this could mean famine and loss of life, it is more likely these days to be interpreted either as loneliness or as stagnation and a hint that you get back to the real world quickly.

VALLEYS

 Valleys are regarded as green and pleasant places to find oneself and they usually foretell great improvements in your life. They are somewhere to relax and contemplate the future for a moment before pushing forward and expanding opportunities.

BRIDGES IN DREAMS ARE OBVIOUS
SYMBOLS OF TRANSITION AS THEY UNITE
TWO PREVIOUSLY SEPARATED PLACES.

CLIFFS

 Many people associate cliffs with danger, falling out of control, perhaps even death itself, but to find them in a dream is more likely to suggest that you have reached a point in your real life where a change is imminent or that you need to re-evaluate the way you think and work. Jumping or being pushed over the cliff will not destroy you: it is forcing you to accept that a radical change is now essential, one that is beneficial if taken thoughtfully.

BRIDGES

 Bridges and crossings often indicate a change. This is a time of transition, a possibility of new growth or a new direction.

CROSSROADS

To dream of finding yourself at a crossroads has long been regarded as a sign that an important decision lies in store. Be prepared for this to present itself and allow intuition to guide you in your choice.

WATER

Dream researchers have always interpreted water as symbolizing the emotional side of our nature but it can also represent rebirth.

IF YOU DREAM OF THE OCEAN YOU ARE DREAMING
OF LIFE ITSELF, WITH ALL ITS POWERFUL EMOTIONS.

THE SEA

 An ocean or sea represents life itself. The waves in the sea are representative of our emotions and reflect our inner turmoil or calm accordingly. A shallow sea suggests superficiality, whereas a rough sea suggests uncontrollable and extremely powerful emotions, a calm sea suggests tranquillity.

RIVERS

 A river or stream usually represents the course of your life. If it is clear, smooth, and flowing, it is likely that prosperity surrounds you or is approaching. If you are swimming against the flow or trying to cross it at a dangerous point, stop reconsider your actions and try to follow an easier route.

LAKES

 If the water of the lake is smooth, it should mirror your life rhythms, but if it is choppy and turbulent, you should take action to return it to peace and equanimity: pour oil on troubled waters.

POOLS

 Dreaming of looking into a pool may suggest that we need to use it like a mirror, to reflect our problem back to us in order to correct it. A swimming pool suggests that we should seek relaxation and possibly that we need to sort out our emotional relationships. A pool of water or puddle is usually seen as an irritating problem that affects you emotionally. If you want to mop it up, you may feel that it is foolish or inappropriate; if you walk around it, you may not be able to face the implications.

WASHING

 Washing or bathing suggests a spiritual cleansing in order to get rid of negative emotions. It represents a "baptism" into a new way of living and thinking.

TEARS

 Tears of joy or sorrow represent an emotional cleansing leading to greater spiritual awareness and compassion. If we dream of making someone else cry, we should examine our own conduct carefully.

DROWNING

Dreams of drowning are very common. Older interpretations of such dreams suggested loss of life or property but we now see them as a clear warning that you are being overwhelmed and that you are not in control of the situation. You must relax and view your problems from a different perspective or you will find yourself literally "going under."

✳ TRAVELING ✳

Travels of any kind are potent representations of our journey through life and often incorporate familiar buildings, images, people, or places. Departures, formerly seen as synonymous with death, are interpreted now as opportunities for new beginnings. Arrivals are viewed as the successful completion of a project or goal.

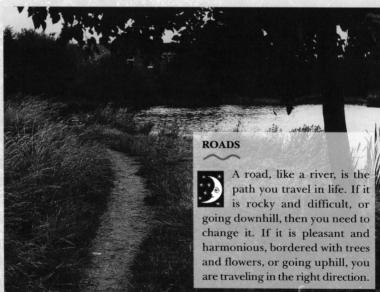

ROADS

A road, like a river, is the path you travel in life. If it is rocky and difficult, or going downhill, then you need to change it. If it is pleasant and harmonious, bordered with trees and flowers, or going uphill, you are traveling in the right direction.

TUNNELS

 For Freud, tunnels were like hallways and clearly a sexual symbol and this is how they've entered the popular imagination. But they may represent long dull paths to achievement, or restrictions of some kind. We think of someone with tunnel vision having a blinkered, or narrow, view of reality. A tunnel can also be a route from one plane of consciousness to another.

CARS

 The car represents the dreamer and is a detached modern symbol which enables them to view their life. It might be swish and elegant or it might be puttering along and badly in need of a service. Does this apply to you?

DRIVING

 This is a simple analogy for the road of your life. If you are in the driving seat, then you are in control, but if you are a passenger, you must consider if this is the correct place for you to travel. If you are driving downhill, this is likely to be the wrong direction, and if the car is underpowered, perhaps you should put more energy into your life and ambitions.

BUSES

 To dream of being on a bus suggests that you need to learn how to conduct yourself as part of a group while retaining your individuality.

FLYING

Dreams of flying are common. Old dream books claimed that flying high indicated marital problems and flying low, sickness and upheaval but modern interpreters see these dreams as healthy and beneficial. They represent the spirit freed from earthly restrictions. The world is at your feet.

BAGGAGE

 Baggage in dreams can take many visual forms – carriers, bags, knapsacks, packages, baskets – but it almost always suggests clutter in our lives. We all carry a lot of useless garbage around with us in our minds, homes, relationships, and so on, and this dream suggests we clear some of it out.

SOME COMMON ANXIETY DREAMS

Some of the most common dreams are those that make us feel fearful or embarrassed. The clarity and power of our visualization in these dreams reinforces the raw emotions raised but if we turn and face the unknown in our dreams, our sleeping mind can teach us powerful lessons in our waking hours.

RUNNING

 Running in dreams can be interpreted in many ways. If we are running away, we are trying to escape from a situation or relationship in which we feel trapped. However, if we are running on the spot, we are afraid that we will be caught out. If, on the other hand, we are running forward fearlessly, this suggests confidence in our own abilities.

PURSUIT

 Dreams of pursuit are common. In them, the dreamer is usually being chased by violent men, wild animals, unseen demons, everything that represents aggression and fear to the unconscious mind. If a pursuit dream recurs, convince yourself before you go to sleep that this time you will turn and face the pursuer. The pursuer is invariably a symbol for a situation you are fleeing in your conscious life. If the chase is in slow motion, it is likely that the real-life confrontation is imminent.

TRAPS

 Traps can take many forms in the symbols of dreams but are likely to be unambiguous to the dreamer. The message is clear: the trap is of your own making and you must make an effort to change the situation.

FALLING

Most of us have, at some time, dreamed of falling from a great height either from a tall building, a cliff, an airplane, or simply out of bed. This suggests that we feel that we are not in control of our situation and should seek a gentle, supportive way to correct the balance.

NUDITY

In our everyday lives we hide ourselves and our real personalities beneath our clothes. It can be quite a shock therefore, to dream that we are naked in a room full of strangers. Such dreams used to be regarded as bad omens, foretelling scandal and shame in society but now they are thought to indicate that we are not afraid to lose our inhibitions and reveal our true selves. Dreams of nudity are always a good sign.

DREAMS OF RUNNING CAN BE INTERPRETED IN A VARIETY OF WAYS DEPENDING ON WHETHER WE ARE RUNNING TOWARD OR AWAY FROM A SITUATION.

✦

THE CIRCLE OF LIFE

✦

Births and deaths and childhood are very common dream themes and yet they do not literally foretell such events and are rarely related to people you know. Similarly, time passing is a common thread, often associated with anxiety about the way we are shaping our destiny.

BIRTH

 We tend to dream of a birth when we are about to embark on a new project or, specifically, a new way of life. Dreams of birth are often associated with an awakening spirituality.

DEATH

 A dream of death can be a frightening experience because of the way we perceive the subject in our Western culture, but it seldom portends death in the literal sense. See it as the end of one cycle and the birth of a new one. Be prepared to release the old and decayed aspects of your life and turn to invigorate the new.

CHILDREN

 Children in dreams are usually aspects of yourself such as innocence, playfulness, or vulnerability. They suggest that you are taking life too seriously and should resurrect the child within.

TIME

 Time can feature as the seasons, as day or night, as a clock or watch, or even as a timetable. Clocks often engender feelings of anxiety because they make us see the need to be punctilious and reinforce a fear of being too late to grasp opportunities. Timetables are a gentle reminder to organize your life.

SOME OF THE MOST COMMON DREAMS ARE ABOUT
BOTH DEATH AND THE PASSAGE OF TIME.

SEASONS

Dreams of the seasons allow us to develop and change. If we do not learn from the lessons that each season brings, we will revisit them. Spring allows us a new start, Summer gives us time to implement our strategies, Fall the opportunity to assess our development and prepare for Winter when we sort through the lessons we have learned and prepare for the next period of spiritual growth in Spring.

NIGHT AND DAY

The time of day has a special significance in our dreams. Dreaming of the morning suggests that we examine our early years for spiritual enlightenment, but nighttime dreams are paradoxical. They may suggest that we are unfocused and lack mental clarity in our lives, but they can also be seen as the dark before the light-a chance to experience a new awakening or a sign of a brighter future ahead.

✳

THE HOUSE

✳

The house represents the dreamer or the dreamer's soul, and the rooms, with their different functions, aspects of the dreamer's mind, body, personality, and experience. Walking into a strange or dark room suggests that you are exploring your inner depths and dreaming of cluttered, untidy rooms suggests a need for you to organize and sharpen up your act. Allow your intuition to interpret the symbols of the rooms.

UMBERTO BOCCIONI'S PAINTING IS
EVOCATIVE OF THE SURREAL DREAMS THAT
WE OFTEN HAVE OF OUR OWN HOMES.

THE BATHROOM

This room suggests cleanliness and elimination, symbolizing the need to get rid of outdated ideas and sloppy habits.

THE BASEMENT

The basement is a metaphor for the subconscious mind and can indicate suppressed problems. It can also represent security and awakening sensuality.

THE KITCHEN

The kitchen is the work area where creation takes place, so it might indicate that you should implement plans and schemes because you are ready to change and grow.

HALLS, DINING ROOMS, AND LIVING ROOMS

Since these are places where we meet other people, depending on whether they are drafty and empty or warm and welcoming, our dreams are illustrative of our need to nurture our relationships with others.

THE BEDROOM

The bedroom is a place of rest but it is also a place where we can truly be ourselves. This room symbolizes a place of safety and relaxation.

THE ATTIC

The attic rooms at the top of the house might refer to the dreamer's spiritual awareness. They can also symbolize the need to process past experience and memories, particularly those that have been inherited.

WINDOWS AND DOORS

Windows and doors usually indicate an opportunity of some kind or an ability to see beyond the present situation. Sometimes, they are an ongoing theme in a series of dreams with the dreamer finding themselves watching events always from a window, the shadow of a door, or a balcony. This suggests that the dreamer is the archetypal observer, preferring to stand by and watch rather than actively participate in all that life has to offer.

ANIMALS

Animals of all kinds feature frequently in our dreams and each has its own special significance. Sit quietly and allow meditation and intuition to reveal the energy represented by the dream animal and take time to identify the symbol it represents to you. It could be speed or wisdom, cunning or savagery. This quality might represent your inner instinct and you must decide if this calls for correction. When animals appear in your dreams, they usually symbolize a part of your personality which you do not fully understand.

SPIDERS

 If you dream of a large spider, this means that good fortune is coming your way. But, as spiders weave webs, it may mean we should take care not to entrap ourselves or others in our plans.

SNAKES

 It is believed that snake dreams represent our need to reconcile ourselves with our intuition and sexuality.

FOXES

 To dream of a fox suggests that you are aware of hypocrisy and manipulation, either in yourself or others..

DOGS

 A vicious dog can denote misfortune and a gentle dog may represent prosperity and loyalty but the dog also represents the masculine side of your nature, the yang to the cat's yin.

SNAKE DREAMS OFTEN OCCUR WHEN OUR CONSCIOUS MIND SUPPRESSES OUR INSTINCTIVE NATURE.

COMPOSITE ANIMALS

 To dream of a composite animal usually indicates confusion and the need to incorporate the good qualities of many animals to achieve your goal.

CATS

 Cats in dreams used to be regarded as omens of bad luck, but we now believe the cat represents the feminine side of a person's nature and should therefore be viewed accordingly in the context of the dream.

ELEPHANTS

 Elephants have great strength and power but they have the potential to be either constructive or destructive. To see an elephant in your dream is to recognize your own powers and the need to use them wisely.

FROGS

 A frog can represent a transformation, from something unpleasant to something valuable and uplifting. It also represents an unwillingness to learn, because it hops from place to place, seemingly without direction.

WILD ANIMALS

 Wolves and other wild animals represent our fear of overwhelming passions or overbearing people that may threaten our safety and our peace of mind. They often feature in dreams of pursuit (see page 42).

CLIMBING

Dreams of climbing can be interpreted in a number of ways. It can represent a means of escape, either from ourselves or others, it can mean that we are attempting to achieve new heights in our careers or our lives, and it can represent a quest for spiritual enlightenment.

MOUNTAINS

 Mountains are archetypal dream images, symbolizing obstacles that need to be overcome or a pinnacle to which you aspire. If you are climbing up a mountain and the route is easy and pleasant, you are going in the right direction and will achieve your ambitions. However, if you are descending the mountain, then your dreams will be shattered. If you are sitting on top of the mountain, you have attained your goal. Mountains sometimes represent spiritual experience and could indicate that a new development is awaiting you if you seek it out.

ELEVATORS

 Again, it entirely depends which way you are going. If you are going up, you are reaching for the stars; if you are going down, you may encounter psychological problems that have lain dormant and which you must explore in order to rise again. Being trapped in an elevator means that frustrating times lie ahead.

ESCALATORS

 Riding up an escalator indicates steady progress in your career, while moving down an escalator symbolizes lack of advancement.

STAIRS

Stairs illustrate the way our life is heading, particularly our spiritual growth. The way we climb the stairs is therefore indicative of the effort required to find our spirituality. Going downstairs does not necessarily imply that we have lost our way but may simply mean that we need to use our inner strength to guide us. However, running up and down the stairs represents confusion and lack of vision and suggests that we should make a decision and stick with it.

LADDERS

Ladders can represent both career success or status and spiritual enlightenment. Each rung symbolizes the steps we take to achieve our potential so if we climb the ladder easily, we trust in our own abilities. If we miss our footing, however, or rungs are missing from the ladder, we may face a number of obstacles on the way. If we slip, we must acknowledge a degree of failure.

TO DREAM OF ASCENDING A LADDER MEANS THAT SUCCESS AND PROSPERITY WILL BE COMING YOUR WAY.

GUIDES

There are many spiritual guides that people our dreams and bring clarity to our thoughts or actions if their presence is interpreted correctly. Try to see through them to the hidden meaning they present to the dreamer.

FAMOUS PEOPLE

Famous people in dreams, such as TV and movie stars or pop stars, represent teachers to the inner dreaming self, despite their celebrity status. A respected senior actor might suggest wisdom; what advice did he bring? A comedian may indicate that you should relax and laugh a bit more.

GIANTS

Giants are usually symbols of great power, sometimes friendly, sometimes not. They represent major forces in our lives that are there to help or hinder us. If they are benevolent, we must open our hearts to their kindness but if they are the opposite, we must turn to face them: there is nothing to fear but fear itself in the dreamworld as in real life.

TEACHER

Dreaming of a teacher is a clear message to us to wake up and absorb the words of wisdom from those around us but, above all, it tells us to listen to our own instincts.

HEALER

 Dreaming of a physician or healer suggests that we need to find an innate wisdom and balance to heal ourselves from within. If we dream of surgery, however, then we feel the need to alter some aspect of ourselves in order to achieve this.

GRANDPARENTS

 Grandparents represent the older, wiser, more experienced, and compassionate sides of ourselves.

OPTICIAN

 Opticians help us to see things more clearly so dreaming of one, or of spectacles, would indicate our need to look at things more closely, with open eyes, and with a greater degree of clarity.

ORCHESTRA

 Each member of an orchestra plays individually but unites with others to form a harmonious whole. In the same way, we need to balance and integrate every aspect of our personality. To dream of an orchestra indicates our need to do this. Playing in an orchestra also foretells faithful love and pleasant entertainment. To dream of conducting an orchestra suggests that we feel in control of our lives.

HISTORICAL FIGURES AND OBJECTS

 When we dream of historical figures or objects from the past, we are satisfying an urge to review past knowledge or experience in order to make use of it now. To see an old man in our dreams might suggest that we need to act with an intuitive insight that we do not normally employ or it may mean we need to come to terms with time passing.

HOW TO ENCOURAGE DREAMS

A mentally healthy person dreams every night and benefits from it. A person who is depressed, taking strong barbiturates, or suffering disturbed sleep patterns over a period of time may suffer dream deprivation that can quickly have a bad effect on their behavior.

✱ *Put the day to rest: think it through, tie up loose ends, and plan ahead*

✱ *Take exercise in the early evening*

✱ *Try not to fall asleep in an armchair*

✱ *Drink no coffee, tea, or cola in the evening*

✱ *Don't overeat or drink alcohol before bed*

✱ *Check that the bedroom is neither too hot nor too cold*

✱ *If you can't sleep at all, don't worry about it. Sleep patterns vary from week to week. Get up and do something that is quite mundane, but needs doing*

GOOD SLEEP GUIDE

A good night's sleep is essential to dreaming. For the common-sense advice which follows I am indebted to the Scottish Medical Advisory Committee's *Good Sleep Guide*.

FURTHER READING

BETHARDS, Betty, *The Dream Book* (Element, Shaftesbury, 1997)

DELANEY, Gayle, *Breakthrough Dreaming: How to Tap the Power of Your 24 Hour Mind* (Bantam Books, New York, 1991)

GACKENBACH, Jayne, *Sleep and Dreams, A Sourcebook* (Garland, 1987)

JUNG, Carl G. (ed.) *Man and His Symbols* (Aldus Jupiter Books, 1964)

KAPLAN-WILLIAMS, Strephon, *The Elements of Dreamworks* (Element, Shaftesbury, 1990)

KARCHER, Stephen, *The Illustrated Encyclopedia of Divination* (Element, Shaftesbury, 1997)

LABERGE, Stephen, *Lucid Dreaming* (Ballantine Books, New York, 1986)

MILLER, Gustavus Hindman, *10,000 Dreams Interpreted* (Element, Shaftesbury, 1996)

REID, Lori, *The Dream Catcher*, (Element, Shaftesbury, 1998)

YOUR DREAM LIFE CAN BE A RICH SOURCE OF INSPIRATION AND ENLIGHTENMENT.

INDEX